Nature Upclose

A Monarch Butterfly's Life

Written and Illustrated by John Himmelman

SCHOLASTIC INC.

New York   Toronto   London   Auckland   Sydney
Mexico City   New Delhi   Hong Kong   Buenos Aires

For Andy Brand, who, as one of the founders of the Connecticut Butterfly Association, is helping people enjoy butterflies as much as he does!

ISBN 0-516-23893-0

Copyright © 1999 by Children's Press®, Inc. All rights reserved. Published by Scholastic Inc., 557 Broadway, New York, NY 10012. SCHOLASTIC and associated logos are trademarks and/or registered trademarks of Scholastic Inc.

12 11 10 9 8 7 6 5 4 3 2   2 3 4 5 6 7/0

Printed in the U.S.A.   10

First Scholastic printing, March 2002

Monarch Butterfly
Danaus plexippus

There are thousands of different kinds of butterflies in the world. Monarchs are a type of milkweed butterfly. The caterpillars feed on milkweed leaves. Milkweed is poisonous to most of a butterfly's enemies. Eating the leaves makes the caterpillars—and the adult butterflies—poisonous, too.

Each year, monarch butterflies in the United States migrate hundreds—or even thousands—of miles in the fall when the weather grows cold. Many of them make it all the way to Mexico. During the winter, they roost in huge colonies.

In the spring, the monarch butterflies head back north. Along the way, they mate and lay eggs. Those eggs hatch and grow into adults that continue to fly north, laying eggs as they go. These eggs grow into adults that fly back to where their "great-grandparents" began. No single butterfly survives the entire round trip.

On a hot July day, a young monarch butterfly in Virginia begins a journey north.

On her way, she lays many eggs. Her last egg is laid on a *milkweed plant* in Connecticut.

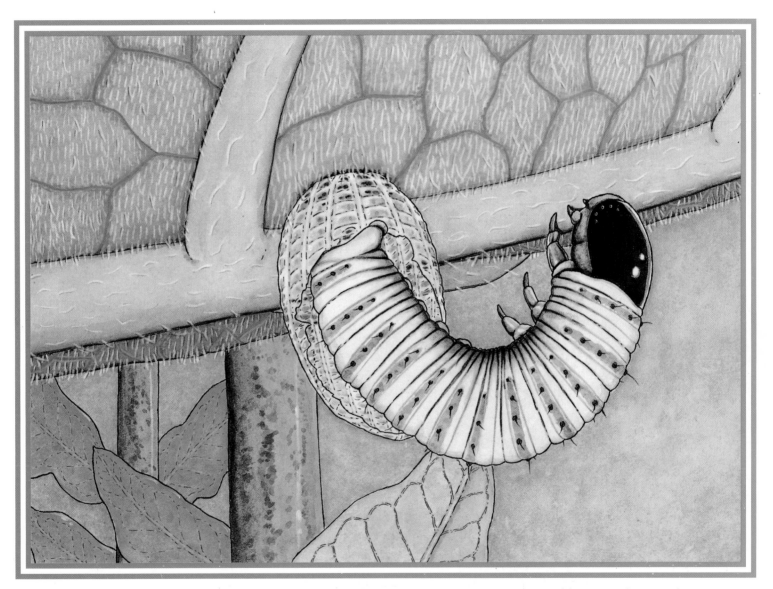

Three days later, a monarch *larva*—or caterpillar—hatches.

The caterpillar feeds on milkweed leaves.

When a wasp tries to lay eggs on the caterpillar, she brushes it away.

Soon the caterpillar crawls to the ground.

She attaches herself to a fence with a bit of silk.

Her skin hardens, and she becomes a *chrysalis*.

Two weeks later, the monarch reappears. Now she is a butterfly.

The monarch butterfly stretches her crumpled wings . . .

. . . and makes her very first flight!

She lands on a milkweed, and uses her *proboscis* to sip *nectar* from the flowers.

Suddenly, a net snatches the monarch butterfly!

The child who caught her sets her free.

The monarch butterfly's days are spent flying, sipping nectar, and resting in the sun.

In late September, the monarch butterfly begins a long journey south.

As she travels, she is joined by many other monarchs. They are all heading south.

By November, she has reached Texas. A gust of wind blows her
into a lake!

After resting for a minute, the monarch butterfly breaks free of the water.

In early December, she reaches Mexico. She has traveled more than 2,000 miles!

Millions of other monarchs have made a long trip, too.

The weather is perfect. It's not too hot, and it's not too cold.

By the middle of March, it is very hot. The monarch butterfly flies north.

A male monarch finds her and dances in circles in the air. She chooses him for a mate.

She lays hundreds of eggs on her journey north.

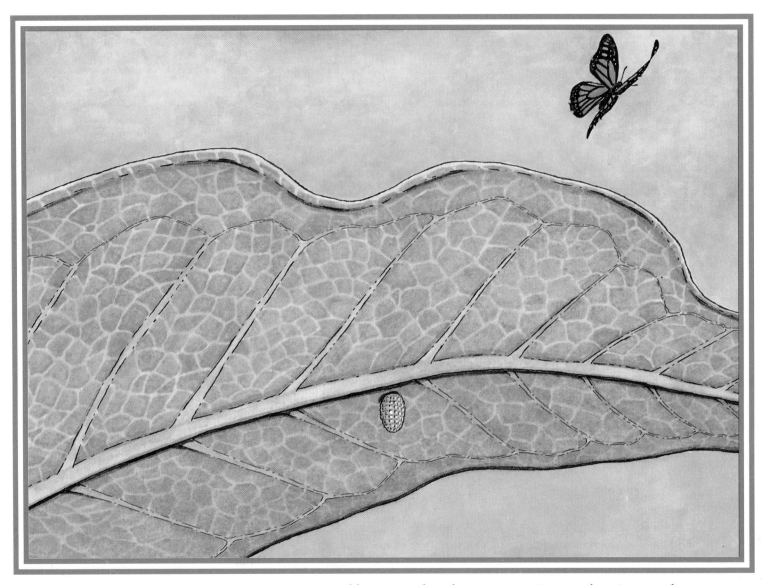

She lays her last egg on a milkweed plant in South Carolina.

She will not live long enough to return to Connecticut.

But on a warm August afternoon, her *offspring* does!

Words You Know

chrysalis—the second stage of a butterfly's life.

larva—the first stage of an insect's life.

milkweed plant—a plant that is common in North America. Monarch butterflies always lay their eggs on these plants, so that the caterpillars can eat the leaves.

nectar—a sugary liquid that plants make to attract insects and birds. As insects and birds drink the nectar, they pick up pollen. When the insect or bird flies to another flower, it leaves some of the pollen behind. The plants need the pollen to reproduce.

offspring—the young of a plant or animal. Human offspring are called children.

proboscis—a long, thin tube that a butterfly uses to drink nectar. It works like a straw.

About the Author

John Himmelman has written or illustrated more than forty books for children, including *Ibis: A True Whale Story*, *Wanted: Perfect Parents*, and *J.J. Versus the Babysitter*. His books have received honors such as Pick of the List, Book of the Month, JLG Selection, and the ABC Award. He is also a naturalist who enjoys turning over dead logs, crawling through grass, kneeling over puddles, and gazing at the sky. His greatest joy is sharing these experiences with others. John lives in Killingworth, Connecticut, with his wife, Betsy, who is an art teacher. They have two children, Jeff and Liz.